BIGGER THAN | *this* |

by Fabian Geyrhalter

BRANDTRO PUBLISHING
320 Pine Avenue, Suite 1010
Long Beach, CA 90802

ORDERING INFORMATION:
For details, contact the publisher at the address above or send an email to orders@brandtro.com

ISBN 978-0-9896461-7-8

Every possible effort has been made to ensure that the information in this book is accurate at the time of first publishing. The editor, publisher or author cannot accept responsibility for damage or loss occasioned to any person acting or refraining from action as a result of the content of this publication.

This book is dedicated to those entrepreneurs who are driven to launch brands rooted in empathy for humanity.

CONTENTS

CONTENTS

FOREWORD

by David Glaze, *Creative Director, AMAZON*

Authenticity. Like *storytelling*, *disruption* and the dreaded *innovator*, *authenticity* has become one of those buzzwords that gets tossed around with abandon, often vaguely twisted into copy in the hopes of riding a current marketing wave and ultimately blurring its actual meaning. However, like all such overwrought terms, the concept is actually based in an underlying truth... authenticity is indeed a valuable brand attribute, so long as it is, well, authentic. In *Bigger*

Than This, Fabian Geyrhalter quickly moves beyond the clichés, identifying key building blocks of an authentic brand and specific ways to leverage them. In a delightfully concise, rapid-fire read, he makes the case for rediscovering the spark in seemingly mundane commodity products and services. Brands need not be radically new to inspire passion, he argues, but thoughtful and honest in finding, telling and embracing their story.

We all want to believe our favorite brands have a soul. Not so long ago, advertisers had the luxury of telling whatever story they chose with little chance of negative consequences. We were willing to suspend our admittedly less-developed cynicism to embrace brand stories we could relate (or aspire) to. No matter that our corn flakes were mass-produced in enormous factories; there was a nurturing breakfast in every bowl...the box clearly said so.

Some cigarettes would make us sexy, others hip or macho. Brands told us what they "believed" in, and we believed what they told us. Activists or regulators would occasionally burst the brand bubble of a particularly bad actor, but generally we were left to our contented illusions.

Then came the Internet and social media. Suddenly consumers have the ability to share their individual brand experiences and echo those of others. No institution, individual or product is safe from scrutiny. Many once-revered brands have been revealed to be not so much interested in our well-being as their bottom lines, their stories simply fabricated to appeal to a particular target market. Banks, cable companies, food producers, telecoms, insurance companies...the list goes on and on.

At the same time, technological innovation has exploded, challenging us not only with an ongoing deluge of new devices and services but also whole new ways of interacting with each other and the world at large. This flood of information and paradigm shifting can all feel rather sterile and overwhelming, even for digital natives. The soul is missing.

It's no surprise, then, that consumers are embracing brands, both new and old, that convey simplicity, caring and craftsmanship. It's also no surprise that this trend creates an enormous opportunity for commodity products. We inherently understand commodity products: a watch that just tells time, a shoe that just protects feet, a whisky that's just for drinking as is, no explanation needed. And who wouldn't be more interested in reading an engaging founder's story than a magazine-thick instruction manual?

The author's genuine enthusiasm for this topic is infectious. I've known Fabian for almost two decades, since we worked together to bring the car brand Acura to life in the digital world. His passion and optimism for the process of reimagining existing brands and birthing new ones seems to have only grown over the years, along with his considerable expertise. Perhaps most refreshingly, Fabian's impatience for marketing fluff and business-speak keeps him focused on sharing insights for action. *Bigger Than This* is no collection of philosophical musings but rather a guidebook for finding the potential in even the most mundane product or service. Expect your copy to become dog-eared...you're likely to find yourself referencing it again and again.

– David Glaze, Creative Director, Amazon

BRANDS IN COSTUMES

About *Bigger Than This*

It is the Saturday night before Halloween as I start writing this book. Outside of our house, mayhem ensues. It is coordinated and focused mayhem: people are dressed up in costumes that are sexier, creepier and funnier than who they truly are.

Dressing up for Halloween is a great analogy for how many educated consumers see branding: a fake persona is crafted to evoke emotions from a specific audience in order to achieve a predetermined goal. Brands don't often try to scare customers to get their attention as people might on Halloween, but in the end the game of dress-up is at the core of much of the marketing, advertising and branding that exists today. It sounds as calculated as it in fact can be, but fortunately this approach is on its way out. Brands are being forced to leave the costumes to humans during Halloween. Instead they opt for complete transparency and engaging, open conversations because of the rise of social media and the birth of a generation ready to participate, as long as the brand's approach is inclusive and amicable. It is a great moment for consumers but a scary one for big brands that are not adapting. The moment presents a huge opportunity for agile startups ready to connect with a large audience in deep ways almost instantaneously.

As I rode my bike down the beach for a weekend ride recently, the song "Moving

Instead of moving mountains, let the mountains move you.

| *SKYLAR GREY, "MOVING MOUNTAINS"*

Mountains" by Skylar Grey came on my music player. The line "Instead of moving mountains, let the mountains move you" got stuck in my head. It occurred to me that the latest wave of brands we love is not leading through disruption and/or innovation. These brands are actually launching with nothing other than a commodity product – with nearly instant brand advocates and huge scale to follow. They are not moving mountains by trying to reinvent a product or service (like Uber, the transportation network, does by being clearly innovative) or the experience one has with it (like Drybar, the blow-dry salons, offering a new experience). Instead they launch their brands based on a different kind of uniqueness: an empathetic story. Their tribes are the mountains that move their brands. They let their brands be moved by the people who love them. It's a

"I hate to say it, but we're all selling commodity. I'm really proud of our food, and I know chefs would be furious if they heard me say that any of what we sell is a commodity, but let's face it: What you're going to come back for – or not – is how we make you feel."

Danny Meyer, Restaurateur & Shake Shack founder
Fast Company, February 2016

remarkable strategy, one that is highly inspira-
tional to consumers and hence aspirational to
brands. *Bigger Than This* analyzes brands that
are not about

shoes
and
socks
and
watches
and
furniture
and
staplers

– even though some actually are – but the
stories that make them bigger than that, bigger than the commodity product they repre-
sent and sell. I'm someone who is obsessed
with startup innovation, the power of design,
enhanced customer experiences and brand-

building as a whole. Noticing this quiet trend made me refocus my obsession on brands that don't innovate on a product level yet are still fascinating on a brand level, perhaps even more so than innovators in their space.

As I started taking notes on this topic for one of the columns I write, I realized that this idea, too, was *bigger than that.* It deserved to become an actionable guide for startups as they set out to define their story and for ventures that need their brand to connect on deeper levels, tell a more engaging story and ultimately stay afloat, even if their product or service is mundane. This is something any brand can do, perhaps with a little help from specialists.

Over the course of this quick read, I will define eight traits of brands that sell commodities and want to be *bigger than this*, paired with ample case studies.

A NEW WAVE OF COMMODITY BRANDS IS | *WINNING HEARTS* | AND IS TEACHING US HOW TO TURN ANY PRODUCT INTO AN | *ADMIRED BRAND.* |

Any entrepreneur and marketer can adopt fresh ideas from this crop of bold ventures that connect with customers on an empathetic level – with no costumes required on either side.

Undoubtedly, by the time this book is published, some of the companies I have included will have changed their approach to branding. No business stands still. Nonetheless, the approaches they are using now are worth examining as you create your own brand strategy.

| **""** |

**An entirely new system
of thought is needed,
a system based on
attention to people, and
not primarily attention
to goods – (the goods will
look after themselves!)."**

- E.F. SCHUMACHER,
Small is beautiful

THE RESURGENCE OF COMMODITY BRANDS IN TIMES OF INNOVATION AND DISRUPTION

We live in times of amazingly fast technological advancements. Every day we learn of a new jaw-dropping innovation, try a new app that creates fresh conveniences, test a service that is even easier to use than the one we relied on yesterday. These services allow us to receive our purchases at a speed we could have only dreamed of just two years ago (e.g., Amazon Prime Now, which delivers online orders within an hour). Many services come with a human attached – someone who actually walks us through every step of whatever product we have just received upon delivery. Enjoy, the company that delivers tech to your home, for instance, comes with a "consultant" in tow, who sets up everything for you.

You won't read about those companies here. I am writing about a subject that has barely been explored: companies that launch seemingly boring commodity products into this world without edgy technology but manage to transform themselves into staple household brands for urbanites and beyond. They are brands such as TOMS shoes and Shinola watches. Their marketing to consumers is not built around new product benefits, significantly different features or a big innovative design vision, just commodity shoes and commodity watches. Still, consumers have gone nuts for them.

These brands strive for what I call the ***AND?DNA***. The AND?DNA is the search for something that was not inherent in the DNA of their offering but in the DNA of their carefully crafted and authentic brand story. When they introduce their very basic products to consumers, the natural question anyone would ask is, "And?" – as in, "And why should I buy these very basic shoes?" These brands can answer the "And?" question with an intriguing, convincing and honest answer that adds a new layer to the brand's DNA: the story.

"And?"

is a question that brands selling a commodity must answer on several levels, and so should you:

"*And* why would a consumer suddenly deeply care about your perhaps plain offering?"

"*And* how do you tell a bigger, relatable and sustainable story around your offering that can turn it into a beloved brand?"

"*And* why do you and, if applicable, your employees devote your time to this particular offering, turning it from simply a day job into a daily passion with all of your heart and soul?"

> # "It's not what we do but how we do it."

The IOAN Team – Wall graphic at the Industry of All Nations flagship store in Venice, CA

Embracing commodities is a counter-movement

to the mindset of Silicon Valley, where it seems every startup is innovating on its product or service or simply adding a new "innovative" feature into the mix. Because of this, one can quickly come to the conclusion that anyone selling a commodity-based brand must embrace the ideologies of social enterprise. That thinking would make a lot of sense if we took into account only the numerous startups that use the one-for-one model, where a brand gives one product to someone in need for every product sold – specifically to a receptive audience of millennials who want to make a difference in this world and do good. That is the case with TOMS and eyeglass manufacturer Warby Parker. TOMS sells a standard shoe nearly equivalent to the common Argentinian alpargata or the classic French espadrille, while Warby Parker sells inexpensive frames. Although I do include a fair share of social-good-oriented companies in this book,

As exciting as the digital age is, the most brilliant, fastest tech **can't** bring what human connection **can** bring.

Jim Brett – President, West Elm,
Fast Company, September 2016

they are only one subset of the ventures that are building exciting brands around commodity products. In the pages to come, you'll read about commodity-product-based companies that create consumer love through stories that go far outside the realm of giving back.

People will always be drawn to brands. We find comfort in associating ourselves with a brand image that evokes an emotional reaction *in us*, and we like to share it so it attracts like-minded people *to us*. By proudly affiliating ourselves with the local National Public Radio station through a sticker on the back of our cars, or wearing the vintage Rolling Stones tour T-shirt to Sunday brunch, or showing off a cool new brand app on our phone, we like to share what we want to be associated with because it formulates our own personal brand. We may be doing this consciously or subliminally, but we are all doing it. The way we brand, the way brands market, the way people market on a brand's behalf and the sheer size of brands people love are all changing forever though.

One obvious reason is the rise of social media. Many consumers, especially younger ones, pride themselves on being early adopters, and they build their personal brands around sharing their new discoveries. That's not a new phenomenon. Years ago, they might wear the T-shirt of an indie band they knew before the group started playing stadiums touting corporate sponsors' names. Today, it's about embracing innovation. Based on the rise of crowdsourcing sites (like Kickstarter and Indiegogo) and social media outlets that report on the latest and, sometimes, the greatest for twenty-four hours a day, seven days a week, innovation is seen as the new norm for many young consumers. Millennials in particular are ripe to fall in love with new brands, so much so that they invest their hard-earned money in someone else's unrealized vision of future products, merely prototypes, just to see them turn into realities. Once those dreams turn into actual brands, these early supporters are running toward them with open arms and are ready to endorse them and shout those endorsements to hundreds or thousands of their social media followers. Why? Because they feel the pride of having been an early adopter. These consumers root for the brands they discovered early and truly want to see them succeed.

For the first time in history, it is more difficult for big brands to gain unconditional consumer trust than it is for a startup brand. We are experiencing a remarkable moment in marketing and branding when brands that either don't have the resources to "put on costumes" or, more likely, don't want to do so have an edge. In response to brands' honesty in the social media age, today's consumers in turn show significant trust and regularly share products solely based on an enticing video, great packaging design or a meaningful story – sometimes before ever having tried the actual product. This allows brands to build tremendous reach without spending a lot on marketing. Still, there's a catch: the initial delight experienced by customers who share a product turns up their expectations – expectations that will backfire tenfold if the product does not live up to them or the values that excited fans are not being actively demonstrated by the brand. Their disappointment gets personal: *Here I am sharing the offering of a brand I naively trusted just to be cheated.* That disappointment will quickly become clear via social sharing, typically through a nasty review to be seen by thousands and maybe even through comments in traditional media.

Consider the well-documented 2017 FYRE Festival debacle, where promises of a star-studded luxury weekend concert in the Bahamas were met with a less-than-luxurious, barebones reality under the stars. Attendees were quick to share their disappointment online and elsewhere, and the festival is now facing lawsuits related to its handling of the event. As Carina Chocano wrote in the *The New York Times,* "We've moved from an industrial economy to a consumer economy to a service economy to an information economy to what you might call a flagrant-exploitation economy — one in which branding and 'storytelling' have replaced advertising and possibly even reality. It's not just that we're being sold the sizzle more than the steak. It's that we're being sold the sizzle instead of and at the expense of the steak." This environment gives brands that have a physical steak in order to sell the sizzle an edge.

It's OK if it's just a simple steak, or commodity product, as long as you're actually delivering what customers anticipated based on your marketing.

As a startup entrepreneur or as a new brand entering today's marketplace, one can gain traction much faster than ever before with the right mix of brand strategy and behaviors but can go down in flames much more quickly, too, as the FYRE Festival's name seems to hint in retrospect. I like to call it "the age of c(r)ash and burn." It is being fueled by the many products and services that enable social reach and a swift launch on the one hand and the easy ability to test products on real customers on the other. Often missing is a fully realized product and a deeper story that connects the products to their users long term. Only those who clearly define their values and their story and embody their passion can strive to surpass that high risk, which can either kill a startup instantaneously or disable long-term growth.

"We are now expected to favor the story over reality, to accept that saying a thing makes it so."

| *Carina Chocano, New York Times*

Branding is just as important to any company today as it was in the past. Customized Snapchat filters have replaced brand logo tattoos, but the actual brand icon remains iconically at the heart of the brand's tribe, often for the lifespan of both the consumer and the brand. How brands are being crafted has shifted radically, though – away from fake image creation toward intrinsic brand strategy, as I will outline in the commandments to come. Clearly,

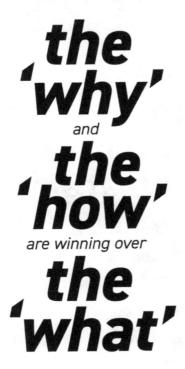

***the
'why'***
and
***the
'how'***
are winning over
***the
'what'***

for commodity brands such as TOMS and are turning into a tangible prized asset for consumers, employees and investors alike. Values are now driving brand creation. "Venture capitalists increasingly prize clearly stated values, ethical decision-making and transparency among staff," noted Erin Griffith in *Fortune* in May

2017. Empathy has become the new norm for any brand.

Although I have labeled the brands in the upcoming case studies as commodities, it is not to belittle their products for lacking in innovation. We can, in fact, learn a tremendous amount from their brilliant brand thinking, from the talk all the way to the walk. When you base a venture on a commodity product, branding is at the core of your offering, and it clearly has to be much better, much deeper and much more intrinsic to your audience than when you launch an innovative brand such as Tesla or Uber. That, to me, is something that deserves our attention as marketers and founders. If these commodity brands can pull it off, how much could their branding knowledge help us in connecting more deeply with our own audience?

When writing this book, I stayed away from

commodity brands that found their way to fame and brand glory solely by means of digital technology. You will not read about the rise of Daniel Wellington, which sells its inexpensive watches through social media, or mattress company Purple, which has won followers through the ease and simplicity of its online ordering and delivery. As far as I am aware, there is no big underlying story to these brands, just a great product-market-Zeitgeist fit. It's a phenomenon that repeats itself almost yearly throughout modern history. The Swiss "fast-fashion" watchmaker Swatch was an example from the 1980s.

I also refrained from including companies that have ingenious approaches to branding common offerings but actually did innovate. Topgolf, for instance, didn't make it in, even though the golf entertainment complex almost flipped the otherwise slowly declining sport of golf around. Topgolf innovates on experience in such a disruptive manner that, to me, it is an innovation brand and not a commodity-based brand. Focusing on the experience component, the founders broke away from the sport's country club image and turned it into an accessible and truly social thing to do, along the lines of bowling. No need to perfect the right stance when you can meet friends over a craft cocktail in the Instagram-friendly lighting and have fun in a slightly competitive environment.

In this book, I focus on brands selling true commodities: products and services that have remained widely unchanged. The primary thing that I believe has turned them into successful brands is their unique positioning and associated story. Their approaches can easily be adapted and applied by any entrepreneur who is acting outside of the world of innovation and disruption.

THE 8 COMMODITY BRAND TRAITS AND THEIR COMMANDMENTS

When someone recommends a business book to me, I always ask, "What was the biggest takeaway for you?" When they tell me, I usually nod and feel grateful for having learned something. Then they add that I should really check it out. I don't, and here is why: if a book has one big takeaway, I usually feel that my time is better spent learning about another 20 books' key takeaways and start implementing them in my business or my personal life.

That possibly superficial, possibly negligent and very short-of-attention attitude of mine now comes full circle by turning into a definite benefit to you, the reader, as I am distilling my recommendations into as few pages and clearly labeled points as possible to make this book enjoyable and actionable for you.

Here are the eight traits and their commandments that your brand can obey to win (more) hearts. Adopt one; adopt many. As you will learn, today's commodity ventures that understand branding at the root level (of unique positioning) rarely stick to only one of these; they connect in many of the following ways with their tribe.

If you intrinsically believe in some of these commandments, if you are ready to fully embody them, then they are not marketing techniques anymore. They will turn into your unique brand positioning within your industry, allowing you to connect on a deeper level with your audience and subsequently stand out in a sea of sameness.

| 1 |

STORY

When the background story is
bigger than the product

Most of us buy brand stories all the time. These stories are often attached to a commodity product. You can find many examples in today's biggest brands, from Dove owning genuine beauty to Starbucks coining a coffee lingo its customers actually use. As Revlon founder Charles Revson famously said about his cosmetics brand,

"In the factory we make cosmetics; in the store we sell hope."

Today's startups continue this tradition in both their internal and external branding efforts. Airbnb hired an artist from famed animation studio Pixar to help align its team around its customer service goals and plans to expand its mobile presence, creating stories of the experiences of the host, guest and a hiring manager. The stories exemplified the brand in action and influenced the way the organization worked, as *Fast Company* detailed at the time.[i]

Stories about a brand are also a powerful way to align consumers around its message. A recent study by the research firm Origin found that consumers are 5% more likely to pick a wine if it features written notes by the wine-maker, and they are willing to pay 6% more for it. That is powerful storytelling with immediate return on investment. Another study by PR firm MWWPR[ii] found that more than a third of the U.S. population ages 18–80 belongs to a group of "brand activists" who think a company's actions and reputation are just as important as the product it makes. "Brands and marketers that are thinking about product features and attributes and neglecting to tell their company story are leaving money and market share on the table. Give consumers a reason to believe in your company, and they will give you their loyalty and their activism," states MWWPR chief strategy officer Careen Winters in *Adweek*.

Storytelling works just as well in the education sector, as Adam Grant, a professor at The Wharton School, illustrates in his book *Give And Take.* Grant tells the story of alumni working at a university call center and how they approached potential donors. Group A made the usual cold calls asking other alumni to donate to scholarship funds. These fundraisers saw few rewards for their calls, with most prospects expressing a lack of interest within the first seconds of the call. Another group started sharing stories on how scholarships changed past recipients' lives. By simply reading these recipients' letters, this group tripled donations. The letters were essentially stories and flipped the intangible into something tangible, the unrelatable into something emotional. As Grant shows,

stories can change perspectives more than any data analysis ever could, and they can even transform a commodity product into a meaningful brand.

Luggage manufacturer Away launched successfully in 2015 by creating a beautiful hardcover book titled *The Places We Return To* that featured interviews with "really interesting people from the creative community – writers, artists and photographers."[iii] The company printed 1,200 books. They came with a gift card for a piece of luggage, which was released four months later. Indeed, there was no luggage yet, solely a book about traveling. Every copy of the book sold out. The success of the book triggered stories mentioning the luggage brand throughout the media landscape, including content by the creative contributors, many considered social media influencers themselves.

"You don't push your product.
You **create**
things that are fun to
talk about,
to **write** about,
to **share**,"

co-founder Jen Rubio (both co-founders are Warby Parker alums) told *Inc.* Today, the book has become a full-fledged magazine titled *Here* "for travelers, by travelers," as well as the *Airplane Mode* podcast "exploring the reasons we travel and places we find ourselves." As Rubio added in *Fast Company,* "It's insane to me how many luggage companies never talk about travel." The unique factor did not stop there as Away took advantage of the popularity of customization (more about customization on page 156). Allowing future luggage owners to personalize their product, the startup hired artists to hand-paint the customer's initials onto the suitcase.

As Shonda Rhimes, creator of television series *Grey's Anatomy* (among many others), stated in *Forbes,*[iv] "In a world of unlimited voices and choices, those who can bring people together and tell a good story have power." Leading with story to make a brand stand out can be summed up as *the art of story branding.* Anyone who has taken a marketing class in college or received an MBA has probably learned about the "unique selling proposition," or USP. Jim Signorelli, author of *Storybranding,* says the new USP is the "Unique *Story* Proposition." Making your brand the hero of the story creates deep emotional connections, the same way as when you read about a hero in a book or as you binge-watch your favorite cable TV series. Through the assistance of social sharing and predominantly online product research and subsequent purchases, brand stories quickly turn into brand gold. They are now the "unique brand story proposition" that turns a brand story into a brand purchase.

Matthew Griffin, the founder of Combat Flip Flops, understands this well. While on duty in Afghanistan, Griffin, then a U.S. Army Ranger, stumbled upon an Afghan combat boot factory that also created flip flops for soldiers for when they were taking off their boots to pray.[v] Feeling empathy for the people he met ("such honorable hosts; an amazing experience," he told *Inc.* magazine), he immediately knew he wanted to bring those flip flop designs home with the goal of creating jobs and funding education in war-torn countries such as Afghanistan. Griffin took the saying "Borders frequented by merchants seldom need soldiers" and inspired his tribe to help that cause. The website now features lines such as "bad for combat, perfect for peacemaking" to describe the flip flops offered. There is no big product or service innovation in the case of Combat Flip Flops, but there is a story that is so much bigger than flip flops – a story that leads to sales. For consumers, the draw is, "If I can pick any flip flops, I might as well pick Combat because I want to be part of their story."

Identifying your unique story can propel your commodity product into a brand. It is the absolute best way to launch a brand that is not based on innovation.

CASE STUDY

FISHPEOPLE SEAFOOD
COMMODITY PRODUCT: *Fish*

Portland, Oregon–based Fishpeople Seafood sells fish for human consumption, as the name suggests. Although fish is by nature a commodity, Fishpeople Seafood stands out by focusing on "high quality, environmentally & socially conscious products." The startup, founded in 2012 to "re-imagine North America's relationship to the sea," has differentiated itself further by becoming a certified B Corp, thereby doing what the B Corporation website describes as "meeting rigorous standards of social and environmental performance, accountability, and transparency." Fishpeople seems to intrinsically have made "story" its main brand ingredient. Based on a mix of deep passion and decades of past work experience by its founder(s) in startups, venture capital, and fashion, and powered by co-founder Michael Baratoff's MBA, it seems to be the perfect ingredient for a brand-forward organization.

But Fishpeople's brand is not just built on socially responsible sizzle. What makes its story authentic is its simple "trace your fish" functionality, which allows consumers to "meet the fishermen who put people in Fishpeople" via a code on the product package that, plugged into its website, reveals all you ever wanted to know about the origin of the piece of fish you are about to enjoy. Consumers can find out for themselves the exact place a fish was caught, by whom and on what boat – all information that creates peace of mind and a vivid story about the food on their plates. "People want to know where their food is coming from," CEO Ken Plasse told me in an e-mail interview for this book. "They want to know how it was handled and what effect raising, catching, processing, packaging and delivering that food has on the environment. We see this across the country from people who go to their local farmers' markets and in those who spend an increasing amount of time reading product labels at the grocery store. This heightened awareness among consumers tells us not only that traceability is an important tool that provides them with a link to the source of their food, but also that complete transparency is at the true heart of what has enabled our success at Fishpeople. When you have nothing to hide about where your fish comes from and how it's caught and handled, consumers don't just appreciate and value that – even more importantly, they opt in to become a part of your larger story and mission, too."

Of course the "trace your fish"

gesture also drives consumers to the brand's website, where (most) brand stories fully unfold. The site includes a blog focusing on "the people behind your food," recipes and cooking tips and the "SO FISH TICATED" T-shirt you can purchase. Once you plug in your "trace your fish" code, you are basically hooked on the brand.

Leading with the story of connecting to your food in deeper ways, Fishpeople is also leading my case studies in this book by not only representing a commodity brand that stands out through the power of story, but further by touching on every single other brand trait I believe can turn even a commodity-based startup into a meaningful brand and subsequently a successful business. Reading the "About Us" area of Fishpeople's website reveals the power of Fishpeople's understanding of all eight *Bigger Than This* brand traits. (To read how Fishpeople embodies every single one of the brand traits discussed in this book, head over to the Appendix on page 174.)

THE STORY COMMANDMENTS

(+) *Go back to the roots of your company or the way the founders met. More often than not, the sheer determination that fueled the launch has a unique story already hidden within it. All you have to do is voice it in a clear and accessible manner.*

(+) *Think of ways brands in other verticals are winning consumers' hearts through unique stories; then see if there is room for similar stories in your niche. Coming up with such a story for your brand may involve daunting tasks such as changing operational processes, staffing, the way you source product or the location where you work or deliver what you sell. If the* *change supports or even builds a bigger brand story, your short-term loss will be rewarded in the long term.*

➕ *Make your unique story the backbone of your brand's positioning, and keep talking the talk, followed by sincerely walking the walk.*

➕ *If you have a good story, weave it into everything you say and everything you do. It's not an annoyance to your audience. It's your brand glue that holds it all together. Let the world form an opinion based on your repeat actions supporting your honest story, and your audience will turn into brand adopters and advocates. This is different from shouting what you want them to buy into from a soapbox, which will turn them off and ultimately bore them.*

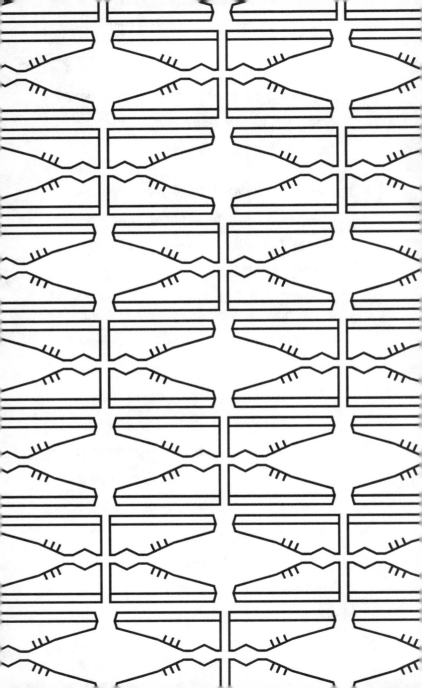

| 2 |

BELIEF

When values are
bigger than the product

The financial crisis of 2008 led to uncertainty and unemployment, which led to people losing trust not only in big banks but in other large corporations, too. Not coincidentally, people went frugal and started crafting and cooking again, preferring local eateries and buying artisanal products. Many small brands were born out of consumers' desire to associate with those they could trust. New tribes formed based on a desire for honest products crafted by honest people – people they can trust.

We are still feeling the repercussions of this shift. Today, we are seeing the biggest of brands distancing themselves openly from politicians whose values don't align with those of their brand. "While companies are naturally designed to be moneymaking enterprises, they are adapting to meet new social and political expectations in sometimes startling ways," David Gelles states in *The New York Times.*[vi] Even Fortune 500 companies understand they have to stay true to their tribe and the values supporters bought into. Today, it is a bigger risk not to speak up. One of the biggest brand rules of all time is "Do not talk politics." This all went out the window, sparked by a divided America in the 2016 elections and the resulting controversial leadership of Donald Trump. Meanwhile, Brexit took place the same year in Great Britain. The largest consumer brands from Nike,

Starbucks, Airbnb, Apple and Amazon to Uber and Microsoft all spoke out against Trump's immigration reform. Nordstrom and Neiman Marcus pulled Ivanka Trump's fashion line. Coca-Cola, Airbnb and even Budweiser aired commercials supporting diversity in obvious opposition to POTUS' ideologies. REI's CEO, Jerry Stritzke, spoke out publicly against immigration reform as well as the plan to review 100,000 acres of public lands and urged people to write Secretary Ryan Zinke to keep the protections in place.

These brands are vocal because it is expected of them by today's consumers.

Their message:

We are in this together. We share the same beliefs.

A day after Starbucks pledged to hire 10,000 refugees, the Twitter hashtag #BoycottStarbucks was trending. Despite any lost sales, Starbucks' decision was a risk well worth taking. The brand had to take a stand in support of the values it shares with the core demographic it serves.

Any brand can stand for something meaningful, but to do that, it has to define and embody its values. Ideally, these values will align with the values of not only its customers and clients, but also the community and the brand's contributions to it. You and the company have to intentionally "live the story that embodies the brand's values," local business advocate DW Ferrell, CEO and co-founder of *Localism!*, told me in an interview I conducted for Forbes.com. To do that, Ferrell suggests asking yourself, "How will you align profit and purpose? How will your model support your mission?" Part of this entails creating your own vernacular and defining your terms. When you do this and share it publicly with your community, members who share your views will celebrate your values; others may go elsewhere. This forces you to hold yourself accountable. You are saying, "This is our ideal, our identity. Does it resonate with you? Great.

We now need to be true to *you,* because *you* are behind us.

Aspiration, a financial services firm in Marina del Rey, California, is a brand built on empathy that not only expresses its values but also is using its belief to try to disrupt an industry. Its tagline is "A financial firm you can fall in love with. Banking and investing that puts you and your conscience first." Aspiration donates a dime of every dollar earned to charities that bring economic opportunity to struggling Americans. It does this with a spin that connects deeply with today's Zeitgeist by focusing on being "the financial firm for all" that invests only in "good." It also uses the "Pay What Is Fair" model (see more on page 152). Customers get to be part of all of that while being able to use any ATM in the world free of charge. Too good to be true? That remains to be seen, but given the mindset of the next generation (as well as my own, Generation X), this is a belief well worth nurturing.

Two very different values – nurture and nourishment – are at the heart of Australia's "first rescued food supermarket," OzHarvest Market, a nonprofit venture. It puts food that is past its expiration date and would otherwise go to waste onto its shelves and lets customers pay as much or as little as they wish. Some conceivably may leave the OzHarvest Market with a full bag of groceries with a hug instead of any financial transaction. There's no innovation here, just the removal of sales and "2-for-1" signs, fueled by a strong belief that food should not go to waste but instead go to people who need it the most. It is a belief so strong that anyone can buy into it, literally. Most for-profit brands can't afford to give away what they sell, but we can all learn from OzHarvest Market's consistent devotion to its values.

CASE STUDY
GEA
COMMODITY PRODUCT: *Shoes*

While spending quality time with my folks back in Austria, I came across shoemaker GEA, a beautiful example of how belief can define a brand. The company produces handmade, long-lasting and easy-to-repair traditional footwear onsite in one of Austria's regions with the highest unemployment. GEA's social and environmental record is outstanding. So far so great, but now add the underlying layer of belief: the shoe company publishes a political newspaper called *Brennstoff* (translated: Fuel), in which the charismatic owner, Heini Staudinger, boldly voices his opinions on hot topics such as politics, religion and the economy. He pushes the envelope on a very clear and steady social course, one that many don't appreciate; one that upsets corporations, investors, banks and the government; and one that appreciators truly love. The for-profit company, which is named after the goddess of earth, condemns consumerism and capitalism (even releasing its own currency called "Waldviertler," which is accepted by 200 regional businesses), yet it attracts so much money through crowdfunding that its team is looking past its many stores to unconventional ways of expanding its operations, such as founding an academy. Staudinger welcomes the chance to explain his reasons. "I am not very interested in capital. I am very interested in life," he says in the documentary *Das Leben ist keine Generalprobe (Life Is Not a Rehearsal* by Nicole Scherg, which I found out was coincidentally produced by my brother's production firm, NGF).

Being unafraid to exclude the many and to be extremely powerful to the few is what makes a true brand based on shared belief and values truly great. GEA is living proof that going against the grain and staying true to your personal beliefs, even if they are based on extreme political opinions (or religious beliefs), can be a powerful branding tool. It may turn out to be your very own undiluted and uncensored personality that will turn into your brand's personality, just as it did for Staudinger.

THE BELIEF COMMANDMENTS

(+) *Shared values will always have a bigger impact on your tribe than your products alone.*

(+) *The only way to deeply connect with your tribe through a shared belief is by deeply understanding your members. This takes a lot of monitoring, listening and, most of all, conversing in an open and non-corporate manner on social media channels as well as in person (at events rather than focus groups, in case you were thinking it was that easy).*

Passionate beliefs, if voiced in an honest, empathetic and bold manner, can become the driving force of your business. Shared values and the expression of passionate beliefs will also likely play a significant role in sparking sales and increasing the value of shares as an added benefit.

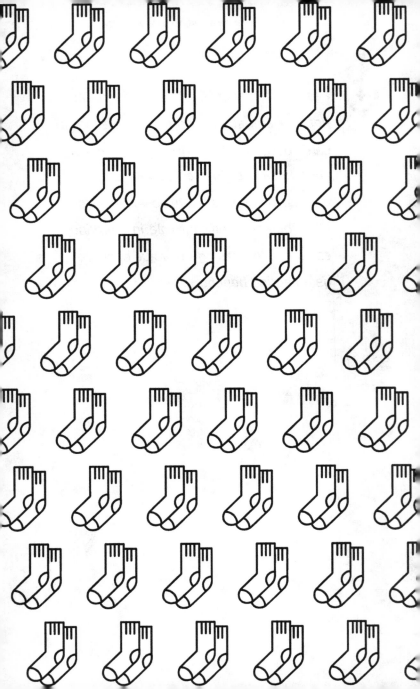

| 3 |

CAUSE

When the cause is
bigger than the product

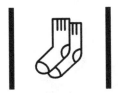

Aligning your commodity brand's existence with a cause can give you strong brand positioning if done truthfully. Will Young, founder and president of Sydney-based Campos Coffee, states his reason for a purpose- and cause-oriented brand in a company video: "If we are not in it for good, then there is no reason to wake up every morning and go to work." His words would not be as powerful if Campos Coffee had not demonstrated its commitment to ethics and philanthropy in coffee by being a Fair Trade Certified organization that calls itself "Direct Trade" by improving education and living standards of the communities with which it works.

There is a powerful reason his approach works. Over the past five years, it has become somewhat of a staple for startups founded by millennials to identify a social cause that can be activated in an authentic way to manifest that the purpose of a product or service goes deeper than solely generating sales. "Purpose" is ingrained in their thinking. The idea is, **"We don't work for money alone. Money is a necessity but not the reason we are going into the workforce."** Millennials' emphasis on purpose is probably why there is even a startup, Pledge 1%, to foster startups that seek to commit 1% of their equity, product, profit or time to charity. As Pledge 1% CEO Amy Lesnick told *Fast*

Company, "In 15 years we might not even exist as early-stage philanthropy will be as common as setting aside equity for future employees."[vii]

The best way to tap into the cause-related marketing trend is to think unselfishly. If you are an entrepreneur considering selling any product, whether a commodity or not, ask yourself why it matters to bring it into this world at this very point in time (and for the long term) and why your audience will deeply care about an often otherwise labeled "so what?" product.

One brand that has answered this question in a unique way is the Package Free Shop. It started as a commodity store (wait, a store just by itself is seen as a commodity by many today!) that specializes in selling commodities such as toothbrushes, razors, soap, bags, laundry detergent, etc. The Package Free Shop is 100% cause-based, selling re-usable alternatives to single-use disposable commodities while teaching customers how to live a "zero-waste life."[viii]

Also ask yourself what your brand will be giving back. Can you identify a social cause that can be activated in an authentic way to manifest that the purpose of the product/service goes deeper than solely generating sales? That is the easiest way.

Research shows how much consumers value brands that support charitable causes. A recent cause marketing survey conducted by research firm Toluna[ix] showed that 39% of consumers buy into integrated cause strategies such as the "sell one, donate one" model used by TOMS shoes. The majority of

CONSUMERS ACTIVELY SEEK OUT BRANDS THAT DONATE TO CAUSES AND SAY THAT THEY WOULD BE MORE LIKELY TO MAKE A PURCHASE OF A BRAND THAT SUPPORTS A SHARED CAUSE,

according to the survey. Millennials top that list with 49% seeking out cause brands.

Buy-one-give-one marketing is just one of the many ways brands are connecting with a cause. Here are some other creative ways startups are giving back and connecting their cause with a target audience's consciousness outside of the one-for-one model:

- Supporting artisans by ethically sourcing products in developing countries and providing them with steady work at far-better-than-usual pay, along with social programs, education and skills training.

- Giving back 1% to your (shared) cause.

- Creating an eco-friendly, organic, chemical-free, cruelty-free model (you name it) as long as it supports a shared cause with your audience.

- Equal pay for women, which is sad to have to even mention still today but is unfortunately not available in most companies.

- Form a B Corp, thereby having "to meet rigorous standards of social and environmental performance, accountability, and transparency" (for more information, see https://www.bcorporation.net/what-are-b-corps).[x]

We entered into a broken industry with a devastating lack of transparency and innovation, so integrating practices inline with the values of a B Corp was a challenge that we were eager to take on. That challenge has rewarded us in multiple ways, including the strong relationships we foster with our fishermen, our employees and our consumers.

– Ken Plasse, CEO, Fishpeople

- Hire staff deemed "unemployable" because of stigmatized health conditions, impairments or felony convictions, and provide a second chance.

- Run a co-op, owned by your employees or your customers.

Of course, no matter what method you choose, your cause has to create true value for the recipients (both the consumer *as well* as the less-fortunate beneficiary). It's also important to think all the way to the production of your products. Bennison, for instance, has "mothers in Peru" craft its "one-for-one" line of children's wear.

But don't just jump on the bandwagon until you've really considered all of the implications of cause-related marketing. Not everyone believes that utilizing cause in a business as an underlying foundation is a good thing.

Kevin O'Leary (of *Shark Tank* TV fame) is a skeptic. "Modifying the corporate model to solve all of society's problems is simply un-American," he ranted in an *Inc.* interview[xi] in March 2016. "We don't need more companies trying to solve social problems. We need businesses to return more capital to their owners so they can do what they have always done – pass it forward."

He has a point. There's also value in turning a profit and simply donating to charity. Applying the simple principle of "buy-one-give-one" (or BOGO) to everything in the kitchen sink gets tiring and has a tendency to feel more like a marketing stunt than a true-to-the-heart foundation of a business if it's not authentic to your brand. Cinnamon Janzer and Lauren Weinstein put it in even harsher words in an article[xii] in *Fast Company* in 2015: "In reality, companies engaging in buy-to-give efforts are in the business of selling ego boosts disguised as social change, popularized by our ability to craft the appearance of an altruistic persona by placing TOMS shoes on our feet, artisanal jewelry made from disenfranchised women around our necks, and carefully curated images on our social media accounts." Recognizing that the buy-one-give-one model does not get to the very root of social issues such as poverty, more social enterprises are using "new and improved" models, according to the site responsibuys. "In fact, they are often now categorized into three types: 1.0 companies that treat symptoms, 2.0 companies that treat causes, and 3.0 companies that restore," states the site.[xiii]

Sometimes, cause-related marketing misfires when a brand doesn't consider how its way of expressing support for the cause will affect transactions. When I picked up my energy bar at Starbucks recently, I believed that the baristas had my mobile order confused. I told them I had requested a KIND bar only to learn they did not have those, so I looked up my order, and the bar I was actually waiting for was called "This Bar Saves Lives." How do you say, "Oh, that's right, I ordered a This Bar Saves Lives Madagascar Vanilla, Almond and Honey bar"? It gets awkward, and it shows how the brand seems to be so much about a cause (saving someone's life, apparently) that it forgot the consumer's basic interactions with the very product along the way.

In other cases, startup entrepreneurs solely rely on a cause while offering an inferior product. That was the case with Project 7, a brand that learned the hard way that "the product will always matter more than the cause" by pivoting into great products after launching solely cause-focused but inferior and generic

"OH, THAT'S RIGHT, I ORDERED A *THIS BAR SAVES LIVES* MADAGASCAR VANILLA, ALMOND AND HONEY BAR"

| *Me, at the Starbucks counter*

offerings such as bottled water, chewing gum and breath mints, as *Entrepreneur* magazine reported.[xiv]

Finally, if you make cause the center of your brand philosophy, watch out for what I call *cause-stamping* (think of it as a cousin of greenwashing). The TOMS-branded Apple Watch band (advertised with the marketing message "Give Time") reflects a clear brand misalignment despite TOMS' provision of a year of solar light to a person in need for every band purchased. Unlike TOMS shoes, Apple Watches are clearly a luxury item, priced beyond the reach of many consumers, making the feel-good brand connection seem awkwardly inauthentic when seen on one and the same product. For Apple, it may just have been a sad attempt to buy into a "still-cool" brand ethos in times when the company lacked product innovation headlines. Today's exceptional cause-based startups find a truly unique problem to solve by giving back or by applying the otherwise overplayed BOGO tactic. Take socks company Bombas, for example:

CASE STUDY
BOMBAS
COMMODITY PRODUCT: *Socks*

The startup sock companies Happy Socks and Stance shook up an industry by delighting their customers with fun designs and, later, technological advances (for more on delight, see page 116). Sock startup Bombas instead saw a need for socks that play a different role far from innovation and design: helping the homeless.

Bombas comes off at first glance

as a typical startup on many fronts: viral videos, marketing full of phrases such as "game-changing socks that have to be felt to be believed" and "mind-blowing socks," a hip logo in an even hipper bright pink color and, yes, a one-for-one "giving machine." But Bombas has one thing that eludes many brands: a real social need for giving one pair of socks away for every purchase. Bombas realized that "socks are the number one most requested clothing item at homeless shelters" because one is not allowed to donate used socks, for obvious hygienic reasons. As of August 2017, Bombas had donated 4+ million socks based on a congratulatory ad placed by "the people's shark"

Daymond John in Inc. magazine.

The story of why Bombas is donating socks catches most of us by surprise. It is very logical, yet we never thought of it. It catches our attention and captures our emotions. Since we all want a good pair of new socks, perhaps even a "game-changing" pair if we trust the sales pitch, we are inclined to make that purchase. Why? We can support that cause – and not because we drool for amazing socks. Perhaps, hopefully, they will be truly game-changing socks, and that, to us, would be a nice added benefit, but in the end, the purchase is triggered by the cause.

If you opt to go the BOGO or OFO ("one-for-one") route with your venture, be fully aware of the fact that you need to have a very good story that directly relates to your product, as in Bombas' case, and one that deeply resonates with customers so you don't fall into the bucket of all of the other companies that sell anything and give anything. A few of those are listed on the next two pages.

THE ONE FOR ONE FOR MANY

an incomplete and ever-expanding list of BOGO startups.

ALPHA POOCH: Buy a dog bed; they donate a dog bed to a shelter. | **BABY TERESA** *(yes, really!):* Buy a baby outfit; give a baby outfit to a little one in need (not to be mistaken for a needy baby). | **BIXBEE/STATE** *(similar product/ cause):* Buy a schoolbag; donate a schoolbag with supplies to a child in need. | **BLANKET STATEMENT**: Buy a blanket; give a blanket to a women's shelter. | **BOGO BOWL**: Buy pet food; give pet food to animal shelters. | **BOGO BRUSH/SMILE SQUARED/SYNCED SMILES** *(similar products/cause):* Buy a toothbrush; they donate a toothbrush (or more) to someone in need. | **EVERYTHING HAPPY**: Buy a product; give a product to a child in need. | **GOODSPREAD**: Buy peanut butter; donate a packet of therapeutic food to a malnourished child. | **JUGGLE THE WORLD/ONE WORLD FUTBOL** *(similar products/cause):* Buy a soccer ball, and an inner city youth receives one. | **LSTN**: Donates hearing aids for every set of high-end headphones sold. | **MAISON MANO**: Buy a pillow, and one will be donated to a homeless individual. | **PEOPLE WATER/ETHOS WATER**: Buy water; give water to someone in need. | **ROMA BOOTS**: Buy rain boots; give rain boots to a child in need. | **RUBY CUP**: Buy a menstrual cup; give a girl in Africa one, thereby keeping her in school during her period. | **RUNWAY BABY ORGANICS**: Purchase a blanket or book; give one to a child in need. | **SOAPBOX/HAND IN HAND/PACHA SOAP** *(same products/cause)*: Buy soap; give soap to a child in need. | **THE COMPANY STORE**: Buy a comforter; give a comforter to a child in need. | **TOO APPAREL**: Buy a pair of women's underwear, and the brand donates a pair to a women and children's shelter. | **WAKAWAKA**: Buy a portable solar-powered lamp; they give a solar light to a family without electricity. | **WARBY PARKER/SOLO EYEWEAR/WEAR PANDA** *(similar products/cause):* Buy eyewear; provide eye care for people in need. | **WEWOOD**: Buy a wooden watch; they plant a tree. | **YOOBI**: Buy school supplies; give supplies to children in need. | **YOU AND WHO**: Buy a T-shirt; give a T-shirt.

What if you are driven enough to create a true nonprofit that is less about product and profit and more about true impact? Take Chad Houser, founder of Dallas-based Café Momentum, a nonprofit restaurant staffed by post-release juvenile offenders, as a living case study. At the end of any shift, 30 or so young team members give him a hug, often saying, "I love you," on their way out. "I really don't know how to put that feeling into words," he told *Conscious Company* magazine. The young people partake in one-year paid internships that further provide life and social skills.[xv]

Regardless of how far you are willing to go, here is what you can take with you as you launch a brand built on the foundation of cause:

THE CAUSE COMMANDMENTS

(+) *Base the cause on a logical proposition that creates an immediate emotional connection with your target audience.*

(+) *Ensure your cause can only be seen as truthful.*

(+) *Be certain your cause is extendable enough to expand with you as your product offering diversifies.*

(+) *Consider whether the cause directly touches your (current or future) staff's hearts in order to foster a strong company culture based on purpose.*

(+) *Hold yourself accountable and issue progress reports on a yearly basis to ensure you are meeting your own expectations and to spread awareness of the cause (and subsequently your brand).*

(+) *Start by giving, then move on to fully embodying the cause in all other aspects of your business, including hiring, location, sourcing and production.*

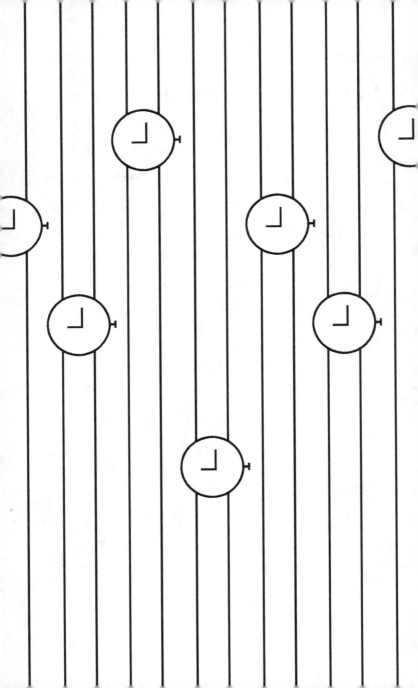

| 4 |

HERITAGE

When a sense of location is
bigger than the product

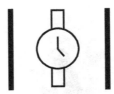

We love to connect with places we've been to, call our home or dream of visiting one day. We sense an immediate feeling of connection and sometimes belonging. Marketing has always taken full advantage of our cravings, from Evian water proudly showcasing the beauty of its place of origin (Évian-les-Bains on the south shore of Lake Geneva in Switzerland – where I was once lucky to live across the lake, taking in the view daily) on its labels to the Danish-sound-ing Häagen-Dazs, which actually hails from the Bronx. That's right – the brand association we make with a location sometimes can be a bursting bubble. The next time you use Irish Spring soap, dream of Germany instead of Celtic landscapes because that is where the "Irish" soap actually originates from.

Fast-forward to today's commodity brands. Formulating a brand story based on heritage can be an extremely rewarding proposition if you can connect your product with the desire of consumers to formulate a deeper connection with the place your brand will be known for. This is establishing its "brand aura."

Just a metaphoric exit down the freeway from Heritage lies a place called *Nostalgia.*

Nostalgia in branding has always worked, even back in the day. That is why Coca-Cola shows us the old Santa Claus drawing year after year while a new singer monetizes our memories of "Last Christmas." It's a new year, a new interpretation, the same feeling of nostalgia – and after 2016's death of George Michael even more so. Brands have always known that we have an affinity for the good old times, for the days that we can now verify were great. In pop culture, we see trends come back in near-predictable ways. Currently we are watching the eighties flashback slowly give way to the nineties flashback, with the best places to witness this being in pop music, fashion and graphic design. We do so while reading books, listening to vinyl records, playing Pokémon (OK, Pokémon GO) and snapping mini-Polaroids.

It would be foolish not to showcase the Detroit-born startup watch brand Shinola as

"*Fans went nuts and sang along word for word to songs that were really not all that great. There was a feverish sparkle in their eyes. They were filled with joy. There may have been some tears. It was a spectacle watching the spectators. None of this was about the band at all. It wasn't about the songs that stuck with them since adolescence. Maybe it was about colorful cassette tapes and the smell of vinyl records, about cool band T-shirts and cherished ex-boyfriends. It was indeed about the memories the audience associated with the songs, about the times they were listening to Blur all the time. It was all about them, not about the band that they cheered for. Everyone celebrated moments they once had, and together they added a new moment to it. Life, as we know, is about a collection of moments after all. Remember the Kodak Moment? Today it is 'Shot on iPhone.' A spectacular way to connect a very special moment that was captured to your brand. Only the most amazing moments are worthy of that brand association. Remember the time you ran your very first marathon and were handed a Gatorade at the finish line? A moment you won't forget. You are drinking Gatorade after your workouts ever since, not quite knowing why.*"

How Your New Brand Can Connect with an Audience Like a Pop Song

A nostalgia brand takeaway after seeing Britpop band Blur live. *Excerpt from The New Brand Post* today's ultimate heritage-based commodity brand. I have been a big fan of the company's story and have happily ordered pricey items from its online shop to support and own a piece of it. Sadly, Shinola stores today look, feel and sound like any other retailer, which is killing the heritage brand's magic a bit for me. When they lure me with limited edition boxes to "own a piece of Detroit," showing me star photographer Bruce Weber–shot locals as they pose with supermodels while expanding their products into anything that can be seen as hip, from record players to bikes, backpacks, planners and everything in between, I have officially had my brand heritage bubble burst. This is a big danger to any fast-growing brand that relies on the heritage factor. Sure, they will expand on their success, but how sustainable will that expansion be with a brand built on the authenticity of a city? Tom Kartsotis, founder of Shinola, as well as the Fossil watch brand, seems to be fully aware of the risk. "I might bite off more than I can chew and create categories that aren't authentic," he told *Inc.*[xvi] in April 2016. "I could still fuck it up." Indeed that may be the case, but not until Shinola runs its highly successful course. Until then, let us slice off a big piece of Shinola's pie as it relates to launching a commodity product by way of heritage.

CASE STUDY
SHINOLA
COMMODITY PRODUCT: *Watches*

Stacy Perman's article in *Inc.* entitled "The Real History of America's Most Authentic Fake Brand" sums up Shinola's handcrafted heritage twist beautifully. The article's subhead: "A mogul from Texas is using the country's least aspirational city as the backdrop for his next global lifestyle company – a $225 million experiment in manufactured authenticity."

Shinola took Detroit, a city that used to be known for quality American manufacturing but became a deserted ghost town in the aftermath of the financial meltdown when the auto industry collapsed, and said, "We'll flip this city around together through providing jobs and creating top-quality American products." Or, as a Shinola advertising headline put it, "To those who've written off Detroit, we give you the birdy." "The Birdy" happens to be the name of one of Shinola's watches, which appears in the ad. Clever. And smart. That perfect blend of heritage and nostalgia is the beginning and the end of it. In all subsequent stories on the Detroit factory workers' lives being changed and the amazing attention to detail given to the onsite handmade nostalgia-evoking products ("A watch so smart that it can tell you the time just by looking at it," poking fun at the tech industry's push for smart watches), it is evident that the Shinola marketing factory has enough fodder to keep expanding into a powerhouse brand that reaches far beyond its origins and that can be found at your local Costco warehouse as much as at jaw-dropping flagship stores in the hippest urban meccas from Tribeca to DTLA (yes, this is how we spell downtown here in DTLA) and on the wrists of former presidents Barack Obama and Bill Clinton.

It all started with a brilliant story about handcrafted products made in Detroit. "Detroit may be bankrupt, but if Shinola is any indication – and I think it is – the story of America's great city's revival has already begun," *PAPER Magazine* founder David Hershkovits wrote in his publication,[xvii] fully underlining how the vision and mission successfully turned into a brand reality.

THE HERITAGE COMMANDMENTS

(+) *Connect with (your) heritage and let it speak. It will create conversations that will have your brand as the centerpiece.*

(+) *Just like attaching your brand to a personality, a location can make for bad headlines. Know the risks, and be prepared to partake in flipping it around as you are now an unofficial spokesperson for that location.*

(+) *Expanding a heritage brand needs to be well planned to keep a brand aura of authenticity.*

If heritage becomes your brand, "buy/support local" may turn into an obvious and sometimes immediate added benefit to your brand.

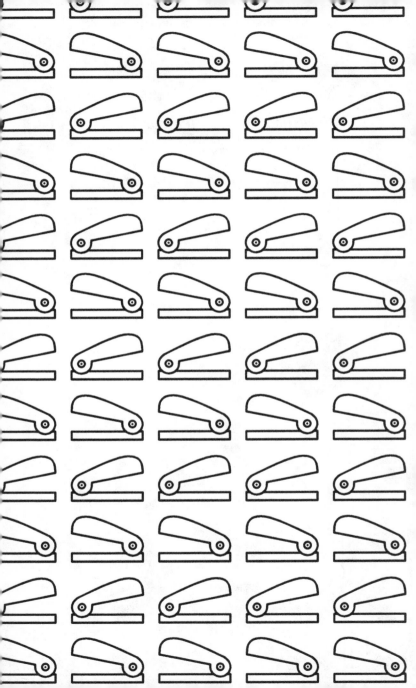

| 5 |

DELIGHT

When the small delight is
bigger than the product

Surprise and delight" has been a catch-phrase for marketers over the past years. In practice, I feel my clients have not fully understood it most of the time. It is rather vague and tough to implement without ample instructions, which often include drastic changes to existing processes and budgets. As a startup brand, though, consistently providing small but thoughtful delights can be the one thing to set your brand apart from your competitors' offering of the same product or service. Delight must be fully embodied in your customer service and the overall friendly tonality of your brand voice, inside and out.

The next time you make a sale, think about what you can give in return (besides the product). If the customer isn't expecting anything additional,

a small unexpected gesture will lead to them seeing you as a friend,

and that's the basis of any relationship. When you repeat that step and that thinking, you move from a friendship to the creation of a whole community.

Chewy, a pet supply startup founded in 2011, is a great example of taking delight very, very seriously, one would think to its own detriment. It reportedly was on track for $880 million in annual revenue yet had not turned a profit as of late November 2016, according to *Bloomberg Businessweek.*[xviii] From handwritten holiday and thank-you cards that spell out a customer's pet's name to providing a 24-hour hotline to ask any pet-food-related question, Chewy sees each customer as unique and, thanks to a customer profile, treats him or her as such. Chewy has artists on staff crank out 700 oil portraits of customers' pets each week; these paintings are mailed out as surprise gifts (read more on "Individuality" in trait #8 on page 156).

Now we are talking true

surprise and delight,

combined with

authenticity and empathy.

It's a winning brand strategy

if the numbers can support the positioning. And as a good proof point that building a strong brand is most often worth more than turning big profits quickly, Chewy was acquired by PetSmart.com for a whopping $3.4 billion in April 2017, which *Bloomberg Businessweek* called a record for an e-commerce company.[xix]

"A millennial walked into a bar" could be the beginning of Punch Bowl Social, which took it upon itself to turn the most commoditized of commoditized places, in bare terms "drinking holes," into a nine-location "fun center" for "hipster parents and their heirs apparent," as *Inc.* put it.[xx] The simple mix of multiple entertainment areas – from bowling, bocce, pool, arcade games and ping-pong all the way to karaoke – coupled with craft cocktails and diner food, creates a delight for 20- and 30-year-olds that is comparable only to what Chuck E. Cheese does to screaming kids: it creates full-

"A little while ago I was driving through Venice [California] and noticed a surf shop that must have recently gotten broken into.

I was mesmerized and quickly snapped a picture out of the car: To me these four simple words so masterfully describe how we help our clients derive their company's true soul. What we are really doing is determining the 'vibe.' A vibe that you can fully embody and that others can fully embrace. A vibe that one day turns into your norm and that you spread with ease. A vibe that if competitors come in, they can no longer simply steal. That vibe is how Keith Moon played the drums or how Craig Kelly surfed the snow. There have been plenty of amazing drummers and snowboarders, but they can't touch that style, that vibe. How Poppin makes receiving a stapler in the mail exciting? It's their vibe. That vibe is the foundation to their brand. "Can't Steal Our Vibe." Street culture poetry that every company transitioning into a brand can learn from. If all fails, if all gets stolen, what does your brand still own? What is that foundation that you can rebuild upon with ease, because it is based on passion and emotions and not products and numbers?"

Can't Steal Our Vibe

Excerpt from *The New Brand Post*

blown delight without a touch of innovation.

Poppin, a startup that has very quickly made it into many households – actually, offices – is a true delight of a case study. Just yesterday I spotted its fun line of otherwise mundane office supplies at U.S. market dominator (and poster child for boring office supplies) Staples:

CASE STUDY
POPPIN
COMMODITY PRODUCT:
Inexpensive Office Supplies

When it comes to office supplies, you either go with the mundane norm or you invest in seriously expensive design pieces for the corner office. Hence, most office desks around the world lack that certain kind of...how shall I say?...pop. Along came Poppin, a New York–

based startup providing us with inexpensive, fun-colored, and customizable (more on that in the discussion of trait #8, Individuality) staplers, calculators, notebooks and anything and everything in between (as of recently that also includes full sets of office furniture) that an office may wish for in order to provide a splash of fun in an often undelightful environment filled with mundane tasks. And a mundane industry it was too, ready to be disrupted, but not by design innovation, which it gets plenty of thanks to product design darlings such as Philippe Starck. No, mainstream office supplies got disrupted by simple delight.

The communication chain of Poppin

is as delightful and surprising as the actual products, turning an e-mail order confirmation into a fun read and opening a package that contains a plastic stapler into a full-on engaging brand experience in midst of your 9–5 workday.

What is most stunning is that Poppin's products truly are commodity products. No design innovation is being attempted. The sole reason for its success is a delightful visual and verbal delivery. It's still a stapler, just one that is orange and happens to make you happy – as happy as a cheap stapler can possibly ever make you.

THE DELIGHT COMMANDMENTS

(+) *Entering or expanding into a visually mundane segment with a literal or figurative splash of color works with any commodity product.*

(+) *Which part of your audience is not having fun? Catch them when and where they least expect it, and shake them up through delightful surprises. These small gestures go a long way in your personal life as much as in a person's shopping preferences.*

(+) *What is the most mundane piece of communication your brand releases regularly? Turn it around and make it* into a delightful experience. Working with brands of all sizes, I see hands-on how little attention and talent gets put toward small tasks such as e-mail notifications,* yet those are the very touchpoints your customers end up seeing the most. It's not always the highly produced ad campaigns that leave the lasting impressions.

Simplifying complex tasks for your customers is at the root of brand delight in the digital age. Map your user journey and start making it easier for them. Don't think only of them; think for them.

*Interesting statistic to consider when popping out those e-mails: e-mail has a median return on investment (ROI) of 122% – more than four times higher than other marketing formats, including social media, direct mail and paid search.[xxi]

| 6 |

TRANS-
PARENCY

When trust is
bigger than the product

"I SAW MORE HONESTY ON A MATCH.COM AD THAN ON AT&T'S COVERAGE MAP."

| *CEO John Legere, T-Mobile*

Some of us, especially seasoned marketers of a certain age, might recall when car rental company Avis launched its famous campaign stating to the public that it clearly wasn't number one. Hertz was. The campaign simply read, "Avis. We try harder," which successfully turned being second place into an empathetic advantage driven by sheer brand transparency, a move unheard of in the 1960s.

Fast-forward to today and a whole slew of brands are succeeding in building successful marketing campaigns around transparency: "Nothing to hide" is the motto by which T-Mobile got its second life. Being the "Un-carrier" is the way the company dubbed it. Through the help of a new, (radically) outspoken CEO, John Legere, the wireless plan company (selling highly commoditized products) started aggressively trash-talking and calling out its rivals (namely AT&T and Verizon) on their pricing tricks, a rather big no-no in the corporate league. Legere quickly learned that "customers hated being locked into contracts, hated being gouged by extra fees for things they didn't understand or couldn't fully control, such as data and roaming," as he put it in *Harvard Business Review*.[xxii] "I saw more honesty on a Match.com ad than on AT&T's coverage maps," concluded Legere, and so the "Un-carrier" was born. T-Mobile gained market share by being fully transparent and running what one may call a "no BS" organization that an audience in pain ached for badly. Now, T-Mobile is not a startup company in any way, shape or form, but thanks to Legere's flipping the company on its head and right back on its feet to aim for the pole position, I see genuine startup spirit within the T-Mobile brand.

A true startup brand that successfully embodies transparency is Glossier. The website creates beauty products by asking its tribe what ingredients they would like to see in any specific product, hence fostering a conversation that is rooted in transparency and care. "[Glossier] asks, it listens and it churns out a new product every six to eight weeks" CEO and former fashion blogger Emily Weiss told *Entrepreneur.*[xxiii] Glossier also does not stay away from featuring competitors' brands on their social media channels: "Where most beauty companies have tried to ignore the fact that women are in an open relationship with beauty brands, we have embraced that," Weiss told *Fast Company.*[xxiv]

The honesty *seems to be* paying off *big-time:*

"In less than three years, and with just 24 products that range in price from $12 to $35, the startup has become one of the industry's biggest disruptors," *Entrepreneur* wrote. "Revenues are up 600 percent year over year and the brand has tripled its active customer count over the past 12 months."[xxv] It takes a commitment to honesty – not only toward your customer but also toward yourself as a founder,

CEO or CMO – to truthfully analyze your audience in order to define important key brand traits, as Weiss did in actively going after consumer input, and to have the determination to act upon it.

If you are in a space known for opacity and complexity, transparency can go quite a long way with your audience. Ritual, a Los Angeles–based seller of vitamins, insists on a clean supply chain and keeps itself honest by listing details on the origins and manufacturers of its ingredients and clinical trials on its website. As a brand that sells vegan, dye-free, sugar-free, gluten-free, non-GMO and dairy-free products, Ritual applied the rule of transparency because it knows its niche customers care deeply about that information and the notion that the company's values align with what they themselves stand for.

For brands founded by a desire for honesty,

going full-on transparent is a path to success that takes a fair share of moxie. If you commit to leading with honesty, understand that there is no way back. If you have committed to sharing your financial statements publicly on your website in 2018, for example, going quiet in 2019 will backfire.

CASE STUDY
EVERLANE
COMMODITY PRODUCT: *Apparel*

Everlane sells clothes online. The twist? Shoppers get to understand everything about the piece of fashion they are interested in purchasing. I am not simply talking about size, fabric and designer bios. Everlane's CEO and founder Michael Preysman's philosophy is deeply rooted in telling all: "We stand behind factory transparency and back up the story of each piece of clothing with real data," he told *Adweek*.[xxvi] "People are more aware how clothes are made today, because of social media, and, as a result, they know what the dark side is. The more information we can provide about our process, the more clear it is to the consumer why the decision they're making is better for the planet."

The brand not only lists all materials and labor involved – from photos of the factory floors to images of the workers making each garment – but also shares costs involved in every aspect along the way, which make it a true poster child of a commodity brand that is leading through complete transparency. The start-up brand even developed its own framework for auditing and rating its factories.[xxvii] Pushing transparency into "radical transparency" last fall, the online retailer shaved $25 off its best-selling cashmere crew, citing lower production costs.[xxviii] This is one sure way to create consumer love.

THE TRANSPARENCY COMMANDMENTS

(+) *Reveal it all. It's the only way to showcase transparency in a flash. Customers will instantaneously trust your brand and its products over your competitors'.*

(+) *Commit fully. If you go down that brand trait road, know that it's a one-way path without an option to make any U-turns.*

(+) *Know that your product and audience ache for transparency if your specific vertical has been known not to be truthful. (For instance, if you work in the fashion industry, which has had scandals about the use of sweatshops in its supply chain, mention where garments are being made. If you run a financial company, mention how it uses funds. If you sell a food product, answer consumers' questions about what ingredients are in it.)*

 Create a strategic plan on how far you will take the idea of transparency and where your brand will draw the line. Measure it against projected ROI, and promote only the most important areas of transparency while the others on your green-lighted list become brand surprises for continued storytelling and tribe delight.

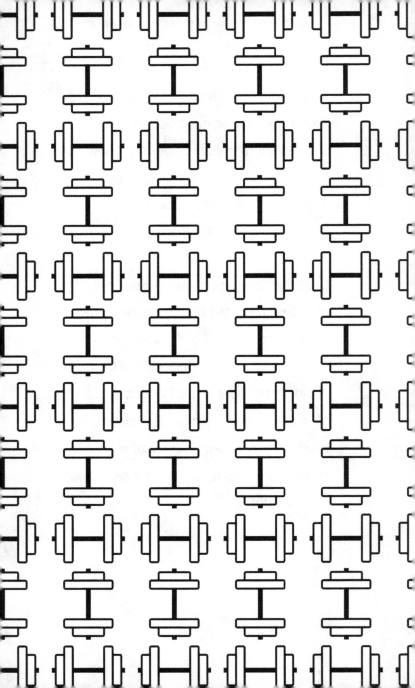

| 7 |

SOLIDARITY

When solidarity is
bigger than the product

Popcorn Palace sells its popcorn mainly to fundraisers who keep an astonishing 50% of its sales. Competitors let their own fundraisers keep only 30% to 40% of their sales. So why does Popcorn Palace pay its own so much more? It has made fundraisers its primary distribution channel and its main cause, upping the amount it lets customers keep while instantly, and logically, turning into a fundraising darling. It took Popcorn Palace a while to craft this winning strategy, but the idea of aligning a commodity brand empathetically with someone else's dream is a move many startups are discovering.

It takes the unique ability to show deep empathy for a very specific, often niche audience and to align your offering, your story and your belief (your messaging) around your followers' point of view.

This is *about* them, not only *for* them. Your brand becomes the enabler of their goals.

Ride-sharing startup Careem is winning the app rivalry over Uber in the Middle East, and much of it can be attributed to solidarity. "In September 2016, Careem offered sheep *[yes, you read that correctly]*, sacrificed according to Muslim law, to customers in Saudi Arabia. It was a move designed to simplify a tradition around the Eid al-Adha holiday that requires people to visit a local farm to buy a sheep or goat, get it home somehow, sacrifice it and distribute it to friends, family and the needy," wrote Parmy Olson for *Forbes*. [xxix] "Careem made sure the meat was divided according to custom: a box for you, one for family and friends, and one for charity. After some customers said they wanted live sheep so their kids could play with it beforehand, Careem mobilized a fleet of pickup trucks for the job."

Can't relate to goat sacrifices? That is exactly the point. Entrepreneurs will never be able to launch a meaningful brand without showing empathy for their audience, but with solidarity, they are going beyond and entering mutuality, and that is exactly what Careem's team nailed with its gestures. You may call the goat story a "campaign," but campaigns can't touch people's hearts long term. Only deep and honest empathy will. As legendary actor Alan Alda recently told *Entrepreneur* magazine, "I thought of selling as manipulating people, because that's how I had been sold, and I really resented that. But I eventually figured out that focusing on the other person's needs and not my own was the most effective way to make a sale."[xxx]

For Careem, that seems to be the heartbeat of the brand, a true differentiator from competitor Uber, a brand that recently became known for showing less than empathetic behavior toward its drivers and employees.

Dating apps are a low-hanging-fruit example of solidarity-driven brands, yet they draw a great overarching picture of the concept at the heart of solidarity branding. They carve out their audience based on niche solidarity rather than innovation. Examples range from Salad Match (you got it, a shared passion for salads) to High There, which is coupling singles based on their passion to get high as a kite. Indeed, the sky is the limit, but that focus is what makes brands that home in on their micro-tribe so successful.

On July 7 (7/7), the Way Station bar in New York offered its female patrons any drink for just 77 cents on the dollar. Here's where empathy and authenticity hit the branding jackpot: the business, noted DNAinfo New York, recognized the difference between the average pay of women and men (77 cents on the dollar, according to the U.S. Department of Labor). [xxxi] *As the business owners understood, the markup lost in that missing 23% can be made up in many other ways.*

Looking at the one-day promotion by the Brooklyn bar made me wonder why the 23% discount should not turn into the next one-for-one model for other businesses. If your brand is seriously concerned about gender pay inequality, look for your own way to emulate it. Just make sure you actually have gender pay equality in your own office before you do or it could backfire. Assuming your business is walking the talk, it should not be hard to attract a passionate audience that will fully embrace and share your brand.

What you can learn from this bar's brilliant pricing promotion

Edited excerpt from an INC article by Fabian Geyrhalter

CASE STUDY
PLANET FITNESS
COMMODITY PRODUCT:
Fitness Centers

"We don't judge" is the motto of this Hampton, New Hampshire–based gym franchise, which offers nothing that any other off-the-mill large and affordable gym for the masses isn't also offering – with the exception of one thing: solidarity.

"Be overweight, we won't judge. Run slow, that's OK. Swing by only once a month, that's OK. Never been on a treadmill? We show you you're not the only one." This Twitter post (06/12/17) signified the brand's clear stance when it comes to not fitting in with the rest of the gym vertical: "Why candy at the front desk?

Because nothing brings people together like chocolate." There. This creates empathetic brand love based on solidarity. It's a tremendously smart brand move, and more so, this ideology as a brand foundation has gained more than six million members who make the pilgrimage (or swing by occasionally) to Planet Fitness' 1,300-plus franchise locations, or may I say, "Judgment Free Zones"?

The commitment to solidarity through its brand motto has proved not only to be highly successful but also expandable. A partnership with Boys & Girls Clubs of America entitled "the Judgment Free Generation" is "a pro-kindness, anti-bullying movement," which builds on the gym's one and only truly ownable brand differentiator, and that is all it will ever need.

Solidarity branding is not restricted to understanding overlooked audiences, it can also be used to enable them to engage with your brand in a stronger way that is trust-based. The 'Pay What You Want' strategy is a great example of not only sharing a belief (Page 62), but also of showing solidarity. May that be an artist (Radiohead, most famously) offering their work for a price set by each individual, or restaurants (SAME Café and Everytable being the poster childs) allowing patrons to pay what they can, and, more importantly in this context, to pay what they want to pay. It's noble, yes, but further it can be used to build a truly profitable brand; one that will honestly and truthfully connect with its customers from the get-go – a brand built on mutual trust. If you are launching a social enterprise (or feel highly socially responsible), and you have the guts, I believe there is great glory to be had.

THE SOLIDARITY COMMANDMENTS

(+) *Study your potential target audiences ahead of your brand launch, and then find and subsequently support wholeheartedly a subgroup's feelings and actions. Will it restrict you? Absolutely. Will it make you the niche leader? If you play it correctly, it absolutely will, and that's often more lucrative and satisfying than it is restrictive.*

(+) *Exemplify the values of your tribe in everything you do and everything you say.*

Be willing to sacrifice profits initially. It is, after all, what many startups do when they build up a massive tribe in lieu of cash. Lead with solidarity, gain fans and financial returns will follow; it's almost guaranteed.

| 8 |

INDIVIDU-
ALITY

When customization is
bigger than the product

Large consumer brands have understood the power of customization for a while and mastered it thanks to algorithms and automation, offering everything from customized Absolut Vodka bottles and Coke cans all the way to seven million one-of-a-kind Nutella jars that were distributed across Italy in February 2017. Consumers gravitate toward unique designs, especially the ones that make the brand experience personal for them. In reality, what brands are selling in these cases are one-of-a-kind commodities. It sounds like an oxymoron, but this is part of a trend called *mass customization.* Today, personalization is easier than ever before and has a powerful impact when executed in a sea of sameness and catered very specifically to a hungry audience.

Limited edition products have long been popular, but in the age of social media, they have significantly more impact. Take Budsies, a Florida company that creates one-of-a-kind plush toys based on a customer's artwork or photos. Consumers send their drawing or picture, and Budsies creates a custom toy based on it. Talk about a unique experience and a lasting bond! Embracing a similar business model, Chicago-based Bucketfeet creates highly-limited-edition sneakers based on artists' submissions, allowing anyone to show their unique individuality one step at a time.

Swedish carmaker Volvo sold all 1,927 of its First Edition XC90 models[xxxii], individually numbered and available for sale only via digital commerce, within 47 hours in 2014. Volvo's minisite stated, "Only 1,927 all-new XC90 First Edition cars will exist in the world, and each one will be individually numbered. More than a number, it's your story. A moment in time marked on each First Edition. Made for you." The limited production run number represents the year the Swedish brand was launched, with each model fitted with uniquely numbered tread plates and a distinctive rear-mounted badge, with customers able to select their XC90 First Edition numbers. Number 1 was allocated to Carl XVI Gustav, the King of Sweden, with number 10 going to Zlatan Ibrahimović, [the] Swedish professional footballer.[xxxiii] After that, you were able to get on the waiting list for your production model.

As Volvo's marketing team understands,

limited, customized and/or personalized sells. When a product is scarce or unusual, buyers crave it in ways hard to inspire through traditional marketing campaigns.

A LIMITED SPLASH

– with expansive waves.

A UNIQUE ITEM

– for millions of recipients.

A PERSONALIZED STORY

– you can not stop spreading.

Some of you might have seen the Swiss brand FREITAG in museum and design shops over the past decade as its one-of-a-kind messenger bags, made from recycled truck tarpaulins and used car seat belts, took design connoisseurs and do-gooders alike by storm. Today, Los Angeles–based startup Rareform is creating similar buzz (you might have seen it on

Shark Tank) by using a similar idea, crafting one-of-a-kind bags and backpacks but from re-purposed billboard vinyl instead of truck tarps. Rareform's story was inspired by "seeing old billboard vinyl being used as roofing during a trip through South America," according to its website and apparently not triggered by FREITAG's tarp success. It's surely a swift brand move: upcycle and sell through a uniqueness factor that caters to individual tastes and creates pride of owning a one-of-a-kind product.

In a smart cross-marketing move, Rareform also partners with artists to create new tribes based on their unique b(r)ands. One such partnership was with artists Jack Johnson and Jason Mraz. Using banners from their concert tours, which would usually go into the landfill, Rareform created unique bags and backpacks for fans who ache to own a unique piece of merchandise. These were smart steps in branding. Whether it be a recycled or an upcycled brand idea, the unique story and customized products will keep winning our attention through the individuality brand factor.

Color gemstone jewelry brand Kendra Scott launched her startup in 2002 and grew it into a brand valued at $1 billion. Her secret, too, lies in personalization. Shoppers make their selections, and within minutes the affordably priced pieces of jewelry are theirs to take. Who would have foreseen a $1 billion gemstone startup popping up in today's age of innovation and disruption?

CASE STUDY
FANATICS
COMMODITY PRODUCT:
Fan T-Shirts

One brand that uses individuality for its brand home run is Fanatics, whose name is very likely to give half the case study away all by itself. The Jacksonville, Florida–based instant licensed merchandise maker has attracted raving fans through branding that celebrates their individuality. Within 15 minutes, Fanatics can slap the thrill of victory on a T-shirt.[xxxiv]

Fanatics creates T-shirts and other merchandise the moment a sports game ends. Employees on Fanatics' "Ferrari Team" imprint slogans such as "Chicago Is Dancin':

The Road to the Final Four" and sell them to exhilarated fans at that very magical moment when their emotions – and their connection to their team and its surrounding tribe of fans – are at an all-time high.

Fanatics connects in the most personalized manner with fans when it matters the most: right before a game or right after a game. Those are the moments when fans' adrenaline is pumping and they want to wear their association with a specific team on their sleeves. Fanatics has licensing partnerships with the NCAA to create authentic brand shirts, authenticity that matters to many real fans. Being able to purchase a T-shirt that captures a big moment in time and literally

spells out the way you feel while connecting it to the very team you root
for wins a special brand trophy in the
personalization game in my book.

THE INDIVIDUALITY COMMANDMENTS

(+) *Customize whenever possible. Start simply by using your collected customer data to create personal experiences surrounding your customer service or product interactions. Customization can start as small as that and grow from there.*

(+) *Surprise your tribe by being personal and hence making your brand personable instantaneously.*

(+) *In order to study and fully understand the individual quirks of your audience, ask your tribe to submit their stories of who they are and how they use your products.*

You will learn how to cater your product or provide service to them in a more personalized fashion.

(+) *Blend personalization and customization, and celebrate the limited nature of your products – jointly, they work magic.*

(+) *Study customization and personalization in your specific industry to ensure you are equipped to make it work financially for your brand.*

THINK BIGGER THAN | *this* |

Most of us want to create *the* innovation brand that continuously disrupts our segment. You now know that having a "normal" product or service offering does not mean you cannot connect with today's customer in a deep, meaningful and sticky way. You are searching for the AND?DNA, the underlying DNA of your brand story, which all starts by asking, "What is bigger than this?" Using the eight traits and their commandments in this book will guide you on your specific path to turning your venture, whether that be a commodity product or not, into a better, more beloved brand.

You just need to feel the urge to move the needle forward to transform into a brand that has a story to tell and an even better story to live.

I believe you had that urge when you picked up this book, and now you have all the inspiration necessary to kick it up a notch.

The easiest exercise to move your thoughts into action takes me right back to the first book

I wrote (*How to Launch a Brand* [Brandtro, 2016]): Use a simple positioning statement to derive the bigger story. Put extra emphasis on deriving your "because" – the reason to believe:

"To [*target audience*]

our product is the [*category*]

that provides [*functional, symbolic or emotional benefits*]

because [*support/reasons to believe*]."

If Fishpeople's fish can turn a fish's origins into a story, if shoes like TOMS can turn into a movement, and if staplers made by Poppin can become a delightful experience, your venture can turn into true brand gold, too.

When it does, **e-mail me** (fgeyrhalter@finien.com).

Perhaps I will be able to feature it in the second edition of this book.

If it does not and you are uncertain as to why, **e-mail me.**

If you feel a brand should not have been in this book, yes, then also **e-mail me.**

These are traits #6, #7 and #8 (transparency, solidarity and individuality) exemplified. See? Many of these traits can be applied easily in your and your brand's daily actions.

Don't overthink it; apply it.

Truthfully,

FABIAN GEYRHALTER

*If you found my book useful, please leave a review on Amazon or Goodreads (or your preferred online resource). It means a lot to me, and it is the **single most important tool** for any author to spread the word about a book. Thank you in advance!* **#belief #solidarity**

| ○ ○ ○ |

APPENDIX

The Fishpeople "About Us" Page

The "About Us" area of Fishpeople's website reveals the power of the company's understanding of all eight *Bigger Than This* brand traits, which was rather remarkable the moment I realized it. Here it is verbatim:

--

What if you knew? You knew it all.
[Brand Trait #6, *Transparency, page 128]*

Where your fish was caught. By who.
[Brand Trait #4, *Heritage, page 102]*

And if it was handled with love.
[Brand Trait #8, *Individuality, page 156]*

And what if all those answers were just what you needed to hear. As in: Sustainable Species. Wild Caught. In American waters. By independent fishermen. On boats with names like "Sunset Charge" and "Courageous".
[Brand Trait #5, *Delight, page 116]*

Ethically. Responsibly.
And you could follow it all, in intimate detail, online.
*[**Brand Trait #7**, Solidarity, page 143]*

Yeah, that would be a TMI zig to the BIG FISH zag of floating
factories, overfishing, habitat destruction and stealth operations.
*[**Brand Trait #3**, Cause, page 77]*

So we lay everything bare.
For the ocean's sake. Your family's sake. And the sake of our
fishermen partners, their coastal communities, and American jobs.
*[**Brand Trait #2**, Belief, page 63]*

Here's to pure seafood, free of GMOs, chemicals or
artificial anything.

Welcome to peace of mind.

--

Fishpeople successfully turned sourcing and selling fish into
an interactive, honest and engaging story. Here, differentiation
started with a story, innovation not necessary.

APPENDIX

RESOURCES

Easily share quotations from this book with your colleagues and entrepreneurially minded peers. –

BiggerThanThis.com

Gain continuous branding insights and actionable advice by signing up for my regular blog updates (we throw in our latest brand name and design case studies as well). –

NewBrandPost.com

Download free comprehensive white papers on topics surrounding a successful brand launch from brand strategy to naming and brand architecture. –

Finien.com/WhitePapers

Need swift, personalized brand advice? Schedule a brief call with me using Clarity. I would love to connect. –

Clarity.fm/FabianGeyrhalter

To work with me and/or my consultancy FINIEN on your brand strategy, name or brand identity design, or to book me for a workshop, panel or speaking engagement, e-mail me directly. –

fgeyrhalter@finien.com

Brands mentioned in this book to visit and learn from, or to connect and support:

Aspiration - *www.aspiration.com*

Away - *www.awaytravel.com*

Bennison - *www. bennisongives.com*

BOMBAS - *www.bombas.com*

Bucketfeet - *www.bucketfeet.com*

Budsies - *www.budsies.com*

Café Momentum - *www.cafemomentum.org*

Campos Coffee - *www.camposcoffee.com*

Careem - *www.careem.com*

Chewy - *www.chewy.com*

Combat Flip Flops - *www.combatflipflops.com*

Everlane - *www.everlane.com*

Everytable - *www.everytable.com*

Fanatics - *www.fanatics.com*

Fishpeople Seafood - *www.fishpeopleseafood.com*

GEA - *www.gea-waldviertler.at*

Glossier - *www.glossier.com*

Kendra Scott - *www.kendrascott.com*

OzHarvest Market - *www.ozharvest.org*

Planet Fitness - *www.planetfitness.com*

Pledge 1% - *www.pledge1percent.org*

Popcorn Palace - *www.popcornpalace.com*

Poppin - *www.poppin.com*

Punch Bowl Social - *www.punchbowlsocial.com*

Rareform - *www.rareform.com*

Ritual - *www.ritual.com*

SAME Café - *www.soallmayeat.org*

Shinola - *www.shinola.com*

The Package Free Shop - *www.packagefreeshop.com*

This Bar Saves Lives - *www.thisbarsaveslives.com*

TOMS - *www.toms.com*

FURTHER READING

How to Launch a Brand:
Your Step-By-Step Guide to Crafting a Brand: From Positioning to Naming and Brand Identity (2nd edition)

Fabian Geyrhalter

Once you have identified the areas of your AND?DNA and if you enjoyed this read, pick up my first book to craft your brand platform. It will further take you step by step through the process of deriving a new brand from scratch.

Find Your Why: **A Practical Guide for Discovering Purpose for You and Your Team**

Simon Sinek

Taking his first book Start With Why *a step further to make us implement our differentiator(s),* Find Your Why *is a must-read after having read* Bigger Than This, *as your head is spinning with ideas but you need clarity to define your own "why."*

Simply Brilliant: **How Great Organizations Do Ordinary Things in Extraordinary Ways**

William C. Taylor

Taylor, co-founder of Fast Company, *studies companies that, as in* Bigger Than This, *are not leading through technology or disruptive innovations but by brilliant thinking. It's a great follow-up read to* Bigger Than This *that moves outside commodities and brand thinking into operations and corporate culture.*

Delivering Happiness: A Path to Profits, Passion, and Purpose

Tony Hsieh

For those of you who have not read Zappos CEO Tony Hsieh's book on how he disrupted the shoe retail landscape, catch up on his unique corporate culture and customer service viewpoints rooted in a brand trait that comes close to Delight, the power of happiness.

On Purpose: Delivering a Branded Customer Experience People Love

Shaun Smith, Andy Milligan

Once you have (re)defined your AND?DNA, this book will assist you in defining and delivering your message of purpose to boost your customers' experience with your brand as well as further instilling it into your company's culture.

Contagious: Why Things Catch On

Jonah Berger

The quintessential branding book on the art and science of making your brand story catch on. Not surprisingly, a lot is based on human empathy, which makes Berger's book a great read after Bigger Than This.

ACKNOWLEDG-MENTS

Gratitude goes to all of **the followers and readers** who give me the reason to write; our **clients**, who intrinsically believe in my brand strategy advice and fearlessly act upon it, giving me fulfillment, joy and purpose in my work; my wife, **Judy**, for bringing constant affection and Zen into my life; my **mum and dad** (oh yes, what would acknowledgments be without Mom and Pop?!) for having shaped me into the creative I am today; **David Glaze** for taking the time to craft the humbling foreword for this book; **Elaine Pofeldt** for believing enough in my book to accept taking it on and for being an editor extraordinaire, going far beyond the expected to transform my draft from good to great (and if you are a one-[wo]man business, I can highly recommend her book *The Million-Dollar, One-Person Business*, which will be readily available via Lorena Jones Books by the time my book hits the shelves); **Jessie Campbell** for carefully lending true FINIEN design excellence to these pages and creating an engaging visual identity around my writing; **Kristen Tischhauser** and **Eilene Zimmerman** for the unconditional outreach help on my quest to find the perfect editor; **Uwe Hook** for telling me I have to start tweeting; **David C. Baker** for telling me I have to start writing; **Freedom Scott**, CEO of Civican (a social network for civic action, which I am an advisor for – please do partake!), and **Péter Szántó**, founder of SpringTab, for being (amicably!) critical MVP "beta testers" of this book; and **DIVISION4 Group** for their continuous support from Vienna throughout all of Europe.

Font Families used: Din 2014, Aktiv Grotesk
Design by **FINIEN.com**

ABOUT THE AUTHOR

Fabian Geyrhalter is a renowned **brand strategist** and the **founder** and principal of *FINIEN*, a Los Angeles-based consultancy specializing in turning ventures into brands.

Geyrhalter is a columnist for *Inc.* and *Forbes*, and his thoughts on branding have been published by the *Washington Post*, *Mashable*, *Entrepreneur* and the *Huffington Post*. A frequent speaker and mentor to entrepreneurs worldwide, he is a Global 100 mentor at the **Founder Institute** and author of the #1 Amazon Bestseller **How to Launch a Brand**. Geyrhalter regularly judges international design competitions and is an active jury member of the **Academy of Interactive & Visual Arts**. His branding work has won numerous accolades, including 32 *American Graphic Design Awards*. Geyrhalter is an advisory board member of *Santa Monica College* and served as an adjunct professor at **USC** and **Art Center College of Design**. He is further serving as consulting Executive Creative Strategist at **Urban Insight**, a leading technology consulting firm, managing the intersection of brand vision and creative digital strategy.

His consultancy's client list ranges from **high-growth startups** such as *Jukin Media*, *Survios* and *Vimmia* to **established brands** such as *Honeywell*, *Warner Brothers*, *the Bill & Melinda Gates Foundation*, *Goodwill*, *W Hotels* and *Evolution Juice*.

Geyrhalter was born in **Vienna, Austria**, lives and works in **Long Beach, California**, and is a graduate of *Art Center College of Design*.

| 66 |

REFERENCES

REFERENCES

STORY

i Kessler, Sarah. "How Snow White Helped Airbnb's Mobile Mission." Fast Company. November 8, 2012. Available online at https://www.fastcompany.com/3002813/how-snow-white-helped-airbnbs-mobile-mission

ii Bazilian, Emily. Infographic: "The Influence of 'Corpsumers' Who Care as Much about a Brand's Values as Its Products." Adweek. September 11, 2017. Available online at http://www.adweek.com/brand-marketing/infographic-the-influence-of-corpsumers-who-care-as-much-about-a-brands-values-as-its-products/

iii Helm, Burt. "How This Company Launched with Zero Products and Hit $12 Million in First-Year Sales." Inc. July/August 2017. Available online at https://www.inc.com/magazine/201707/burt-helm/how-i-did-it-steph-korey-jen-rubio-away.html

iv Forbes staff. "Greatest Living Business Minds." Forbes. September 2017. Available online at https://www.forbes.com/100-greatest-business-minds/person/shonda-rhimes

v Buchanan, Leigh. "How an Afghani Prayer Rite Became One Entrepreneur's Aha! Moment." Inc. November 2016. Available online at https://www.inc.com/magazine/201611/leigh-buchanan/combat-flip-flops.html

BELIEF

vi Gelles, David. "The Moral Voice of Corporate America." New York Times. August 17, 2017. Available online at https://www.nytimes.com/2017/08/19/business/moral-voice-ceos.html?mcubz=3

CAUSE

vii "Why Pledge 1% Is One of the Most Innovative Companies." Fast Company. February 13, 2017. Available online at https://www.fastcompany.com/3067480/why-pledge-1-is-one-of-the-most-innovative-companies-of-2017

viii "This Store Teaches People How to Lead a Waste-Free Life." Now This video. Available online at https://www.facebook.com/NowThisNews/videos/1423893591034094/

ix Bazilian, Emily. Infographic: "What Consumers Really Think of Cause Marketing." Adweek. March 12, 2017. Available online at http://www.adweek.com/brand-marketing/infographic-what-consumers-really-think-about-cause-marketing/

x Bcorporation.net. "What Are B Corps?" Available online at https://www.bcorporation.net/what-are-b-corps

xi Saporito, Bill. "Why Kevin O'Leary Wants You to Be Evil." Inc. March 2016. Available online at https://www.inc.com/magazine/201603/bill-saporito/shark-tank-kevin-oleary-be-evil.html.

xii Janzer, Cinnamon, and Weinstein, Lauren. "The Buy-One-Give-One Model Might Make You Feel Good, but It Doesn't Make the World Better." Fast Company. November 17, 2015.

xiii Responsibuys. "Mitscoots Outfitters: The Buy-One, Give-One Company That Also Gives Jobs." Responsibuys.com. Available online at https://www.responsibuys.com/job-creation/2017/1/4/mitscoots-outfitters-the-buy-one-give-one-company-that-also-gives-jobs?rq=1.0%20companies%20that%20treat%20symptoms xiv Zissu, Alexandra. "When 'Doing Good' Isn't Good Enough." Entrepreneur. June 2017. Available online at https://www.entrepreneur.com/article/294435

xv Dunbar, Meghan French. "Café Momentum Is Using Social Entrepreneurship to Fight Recidivism." Conscious Company. March 5, 2016. Available online at https://consciouscompanymedia.com/the-new-economy/cafe-momentum-is-using-social-entrepreneurship-to-fight-recidivism/

HERITAGE

xvi Perman, Stacy. "The Real History of America's Most Authentic Fake Brand." Inc. April 2016. Available online at https://www.inc.com/magazine/201604/stacy-perman/shinola-watch-history-manufacturing-heritage-brand.html

xvii Hershkovitz, David. "Why the Opening of Detroit-Based Shinola's Tribeca Flagship Is a Big Deal." Paper. July 26, 2013. Available online at http://www.papermag.com/why-the-opening-of-detroit-based-shinolas-tribeca-flagship-is-a-big-de-1427002279.html

DELIGHT

xviii Zaleski, Olivia. "Your Dog Deserves an Oil Portrait with Her Gluten-Free Kibble." Bloomberg Businessweek. November 22, 2016. Available online at https://www.bloomberg.com/news/articles/2016-11-22/your-dog-deserves-an-oil-portrait-with-her-gluten-free-kibble

xix Zaleski, Olivia. "PetSmart to Acquire Online Pet Store Chewy in E-Commerce Push." Bloomberg Businessweek. April 18, 2017.

xx Bluestein, Adam. "How a Middle-Aged Grouch Cracked the Code on Marketing to Millennials." Inc. December 2016/January 2017. Available online at https://www.inc.com/magazine/201612/adam-bluestein/punchbowl-nightlife-machine.html

xxi The Financial Brand. "54 Statistics & Trends That Will Shape Your Digital Marketing Strategy." June 27, 2017. Available online at https://thefinancialbrand.com/66080/trends-facts-digital-marketing-advertising/

TRANSPARENCY

xxii Legere, John. "T-Mobile's CEO on Winning Market Share by Trash-Talking Rivals." Harvard Business Review. January–February 2017. Available online at https://hbr.org/2017/01/t-mobiles-ceo-on-winning-market-share-by-trash-talking-rivals

xxiii Giacobbe, Alyssa. "How Glossier Hacked Social Media to Build a Cult-Like Following." Entrepreneur. September 2017. Available online at https://www.entrepreneur.com/article/298014#

xxiv "These Five Fashionable Brands Have Mastered Content That Sells." Fast Company. February 13, 2017.

xxv Giacobbe, Alyssa. "How Glossier Hacked Social Media to Build a Cult-Like Following." Entrepreneur. September 2017. Available online at https://www.entrepreneur.com/article/298014#

xxvi Birkner, Christine. "How Clothing Brands Are Embracing Transparency to Meet the Growing Demand for Sustainable Apparel." Adweek. May 1, 2017. Available online at http://www.

adweek.com/brand-marketing/consumers-care-about-sustainable-ethically-made-apparel-and-these-brands-are-providing-it/

xxvii "Most Innovative Companies: Everlane." Fast Company. March 2016. Available online at https://www.fastcompany.com/company/everlane

xxviii Entrepreneur staff. "Businesses Disrupting Industries with Their Brilliant Ideas and What You Can Learn from Them." Entrepreneur. June 5, 2016. Available online at https://www.entrepreneur.com/slideshow/294846#0

SOLIDARITY

xxix Olson, Parmy. "Dial-a-Caravan." Forbes. June 29, 2017.

xxx Taylor, Alan. "Alan Alda Reveals His Top Communication Techniques." Entrepreneur. May 26, 2017. Available online at https://www.entrepreneur.com/article/294780

xxxi U.S. Department of Labor. "Fact Sheet: Closing the Gender Wage Gap." Available online at https://www.dol.gov/wb/equal-pay/WH-Equal-Pay-fact-sheet.pdf

INDIVIDUALITY

xxxii Ewing, Steven. "Volvo XC90 First Edition Sells Out in 48 Hours." Autoblog. Available online at https://www.autoblog.com/2014/09/05/volvo-xc90-first-edition-sold-out/

xxxiii Shaki, Chris. "VOLVO XC90: The Full Luxury SUV King." Motor Sports Nationals. May 27, 2016.

xxxiv Novy-Williams, Eben. "Sports Champion T-Shirts Delivered Just After the Buzzer." Bloomberg Businessweek. March 15, 2017.

INDEX

INDEX